Specials!

Drugs

Acknowledgements

© 2008 Folens Limited, on behalf of the author.

United Kingdom: Folens Publishers, Waterslade House, Thame Road, Haddenham, Buckinghamshire, HP17 8NT.
Email: folens@folens.com

Ireland: Folens Publishers, Greenhills Road, Tallaght, Dublin 24.
Email: info@folens.ie

Editor: Daniel Bottom

Cover design: Martin Cross

Illustrations: Lisa Berkshire

First published 2008 by Folens Limited.

Layout artist: Planman Technologies

Cover image: © iStockphoto.com/Lukasz Witczak

British Library Cataloguing in Publication Data. A catalogue record for this publication is available from the British Library.

ISBN 978-1-85008-379-5

Contents

Introduction

Specials! PSHE Drugs gives students the information they need about legal and illegal drugs, including alcohol and tobacco. Students are encouraged to think about the risks involved in substance abuse and how this might affect their own lives. Throughout the book the emphasis is on gaining knowledge in order to be able to make positive decisions.

This is one of six books in the Specials PSHE series which can be used together to cover many of the requirements for PSHE at Key Stage 3.

The teacher can work in different ways. Each unit could be taught as one or two lessons with students working individually, in pairs or in groups. Alternatively, a single Resource sheet and related Activity sheet(s) could be used as required. The book is divided into ten units. Each unit has one or more photocopiable Resource sheets and several Activity sheets.

The Teacher's notes give guidance and are laid out as follows:

Objectives
These are the main skills or knowledge to be learned.

Prior knowledge
This refers to the minimum skills or knowledge required by students to complete the tasks. As a rule, students should have a reading and comprehension age of six to ten years. Some Activity sheets are more challenging than others and will need to be selected accordingly.

Links
All units link to aspects of the PSHE QCA framework at Key Stage 3, as well as the PSE/PSD guidelines for Scotland, Wales and Northern Ireland.

Background
This gives additional information including facts and figures for the teacher about particular aspects of the topic.

Starter activity
Since the units can be taught as a lesson, a warm-up activity focusing on an aspect of the unit is suggested.

Resource sheets and Activity sheets
The Resource sheets contain no tasks or activities and can be used as a stimulus for discussion. Where useful, keywords are given in the Teacher's notes and related tasks are provided on the Activity sheets. Links with other Activity sheets are sometimes indicated.

Plenary
The teacher can use the suggestions here to do additional work, recap on the main points covered, or reinforce a particular point.

Assessment sheet
At the end of the book there is an Assessment sheet focusing on student progress and learning. It can be used in different ways. A student could complete it as a self-assessment, while the teacher or support assistant also completes one on the student's progress. The two can then be compared and contrasted during a discussion. Alternatively, students could work in pairs and carry out peer-assessments and then compare outcomes.

The use of 'faces', rather than just comments, allows students to complete the sheet quickly and easily once the meaning of the three facial expressions have been explained to them. The sheet also allows students to set targets for the next series of lessons.

Look out for other titles in the PSHE series, including:
- Careers and economic understanding
- Diversity and values
- Healthy lifestyles
- Personal finance
- Relationships

Teacher's notes

Drugs in the twenty-first century

Objectives

- To gain an overview of legal and illegal drugs in our society
- To think about the advantages and disadvantages of drug use
- To begin to look at the risks involved in drug taking

Prior knowledge

Students will need to have an understanding of what drugs are and that there can be legal and illegal varieties.

Links to the PSHE: Personal Well-being KS3 Programme of Study for England

1.2 Healthy lifestyles
1.3 Risk

Links to the Draft Curriculum for Excellence for Scotland

Health and Well-being: Substance misuse

Links to the Personal and Social Education Framework for Wales

Emotional aspect
Moral aspect
Physical aspect

Links to the Learning for Life and Work: Personal Development requirements for Northern Ireland

Personal health
Self-awareness

Background

Illegal drug use is still on the increase, with cannabis being the most commonly used drug. There has also been an increase in the use of cocaine. Amongst young people, boys are slightly more likely to have used drugs than girls. They also drink slightly more but girls are more likely to be smokers.

Starter activity

Ask students how they would explain what drugs are to an eight-year-old child. They could work in pairs and then share their ideas with the class to come up with a general definition, for example, 'Drugs are things that affect the way the mind or body works, either for a short while or for good' would be acceptable.

Resource sheets and Activity sheets

You may need to discuss the terms 'prescription' and 'over the counter' before students can carry out the task on the Activity sheet, 'Prescription, over the counter or illegal?'. There are currently no age restrictions for buying over-the-counter drugs, however, many shops operate a company policy where they will not sell certain medicines to children. Pharmacies may also refuse to sell drugs to anyone the drug is not licensed to, for example, they may refuse to sell certain medicines to young people or pregnant women.

Many prescription-only drugs can now be bought over the Internet but it is still illegal to buy them without a doctor's prescription. Aspirin, paracetamol, tea and coffee can be bought at any age. Cigarettes and alcohol can only be bought by people over 18. Prozac (an anti-depressant), amoxicillin (an antibiotic), Herceptin® (a cancer fighting drug) and the mini-pill (progesterone only contraceptive pill) can only be obtained on prescription. LSD, ecstasy and cannabis are all illegal drugs.

The Resource sheet, 'The good and the bad (1)' and the Activity sheet, 'The good and the bad (2)', can be used together to promote a discussion about the benefits and dangers of legal and illegal drugs.

The Activity sheet, 'Pop a pill?', is designed to get students to think about the culture of taking medication for minor ailments. You could discuss the speech bubble on this Activity sheet and talk about alternatives to medication. The leaflet activity could then be completed as homework.

You could discuss the statistics on the Activity sheet, 'Death by drugs', as a class. Figures for Scotland and Northern Ireland are not published in a comparable format but, in 2006, there were 421 drug-related deaths in Scotland and 22 in Northern Ireland, bringing the UK total to 3013. Students could carry out research to add further statistics before designing their posters.

Plenary

Pose the following question to students: Would the world be a better place without drugs? You could hold a brief discussion before taking a class vote.

Prescription, over the counter or illegal?

Drugs have been used for hundreds of years but they are used more today than ever before. All of the products below contain drugs:

- Some are legal, others are illegal
- Some can be bought by people of any age, others have age restrictions
- Some can be bought over the counter, while others can only be obtained with a doctor's prescription.

☞ 1 Copy each drug below into the correct box on the chart underneath.

aspirin	cannabis	paracetamol	
cigarettes	alcohol	LSD	coffee
Prozac	amoxicillin		Herceptin
tea	ecstasy	mini-pill	

Legal – can be bought by anyone	Legal – can be bought by anyone over the age of 18	Legal – can only be obtained with a doctor's prescription	Illegal

☞ 2 What other drugs can you name? Add some of them to the correct boxes above.

The good and the bad (1)

Rising cost of prescription drugs crippling NHS

New hope for cancer sufferers

A coffee break could save your life on a long journey

Soap star found dead – drug overdose suspected

Internet drugs are fakes!

I became a prostitute to pay for my heroin addiction

Man stole from boss to fund drug habit

Trials suggest herbal remedy can help fight depression

Omega-3 oil makes ten year olds extra brainy!

Top athlete fails drugs test

Proud mum gives birth after fourth IVF treatment

Booze-fuelled fight in town centre

The good and the bad (2)

Read the headlines on the Resource sheet, 'The good and the bad (1)'. All of the stories are related to drug use. What do you think each one is about?

☞ Drugs can have positive effects as well as negative ones. Complete the chart below showing some of the advantages and disadvantages of drug use. Some ideas have been included to get you started. Think about illegal and legal drug use and use the headlines to help you with ideas.

Advantages of drug use	Disadvantages of drug use
• Some drugs help to control pain	• Drugs needed to treat illnesses can be very expensive

Drugs

Activity sheet – Drugs in the twenty-first Century

Pop a pill?

Read the speech bubble below.

People take pills for the slightest thing these days, like a headache or aching muscles. Very often, a brisk walk or a warm bath would do just as good a job. Children are given drugs to make them behave and concentrate better when what they really need are a few rules and an earlier bed time. Doctors prescribe pills for depression because it's easier than sorting out someone's problems. People even take pills to lose weight instead of going on a diet! It's ridiculous. No one stops to think about the side effects or what will happen if they get addicted.

☞ Do you agree that people are too quick to take medication? Discuss your thoughts with a partner.

Did you know that painkillers can actually cause headaches? If you take them regularly, your body can develop withdrawal symptoms and you can actually end up getting headaches. In the UK, we spend over £100 million pounds a year on over-the-counter products for treating cold symptoms like coughs, sore throats, blocked noses and headaches.

☞ Design a leaflet giving advice for people on how to treat either a cold or a headache, without using medicines.

Drugs

Activity sheet – Drugs in the twenty-first century

Death by drugs

☞ In 2006, 2570 people died in England and Wales due to drug-related issues. Use the information below to design a poster warning people about the risk of death from taking drugs.

About 70% of the people who died of drug-related deaths were male

50 people who died were under the age of 20

540 people died from accidental overdoses

In memory of 2570 people

692 people who died had also been drinking alcohol

331 people who died had taken paracetamol and/or aspirin

739 people who died had mental or behavioural disorders due to drug usage

48 people who died had taken ecstasy

Teacher's notes

Problems with alcohol

Objectives

- To learn about the short-term and long-term effects of drinking alcohol
- To learn about the recommended guidelines for safe drinking

Prior knowledge

Students require no prior knowledge for this unit.

Links to the PSHE: Personal Well-being KS3 Programme of Study for England

1.2 Healthy lifestyles
1.3 Risk

Links to the Draft Curriculum for Excellence for Scotland

Health and Well-being: Substance misuse

Links to the Personal and Social Education Framework for Wales

Emotional aspect
Moral aspect
Physical aspect

Links to the Learning for Life and Work: Personal Development requirements for Northern Ireland

Personal health
Self-awareness

Background

Alcohol is an accepted part of many people's lives and its effects are often overlooked. Stories about people getting drunk are often told as humorous anecdotes and drinking is frequently glamorized. In 2005, 8758 alcohol-related deaths were recorded in the UK, and the cost to the NHS of dealing with alcohol-related diseases and incidents is estimated at £1.7 billion a year.

Starter activity

The Resource sheet, 'Alien Abduction', works best if, initially, students are not aware that the poison mentioned is alcohol, so try to avoid mentioning alcohol in your starter activity. You could begin by asking whether or not it is acceptable to experiment on human beings.

Resource sheets and Activity sheets

Allow students to read the Resource sheet, 'Alien abduction', before giving out the Activity sheet, 'Alien report.' Some may guess that the poison being administered is alcohol. You can then point out that too much alcohol does act as a poison. Students could work in pairs or small groups to list the effects on the 'Alien observation' sheet. Encourage them to make inferences, for example, when Jake says 'I decided he was quite friendly' this suggests that the alcohol was initially making him feel warm towards others.

The Resource sheet, 'The human body', can then be used with the Activity sheet, 'Alcohol in the long term', to look at the damage alcohol abuse can do. Most of the diseases are easy to place. The pancreas is a gland situated behind the stomach. Pancreatitis causes intense abdominal pain and in severe cases can reduce life expectancy by ten to twenty years. Strokes are caused by blood clots in the brain (or less frequently by bleeding) and can cause brain damage or death.

Georgina's story is fairly typical. Many adults drink considerably more than the recommended daily amount without worrying. You could discuss the Activity sheet, 'Georgina's story', with the class before students write their own letters to Georgina; this could be set as homework. As a child protection issue, you should point out that if a young person is being adversely affected by an adult's drinking they should always seek help.

Plenary

Alcohol is forbidden in some religions. Ask students what the reasons for this might be?

Alien abduction

12 May 2008

No one will ever believe this but it's true. My name is Jake and last week I was abducted by aliens. A bright light scooped me up and I found myself strapped into a metal chair in a huge spaceship. A creature with seven eyes injected me with something. At first I felt OK, quite relaxed actually.

After a few minutes he injected me again and I laughed. He made me stand up and walk across a thin plank of wood. I wobbled a bit and giggled. I decided he was quite friendly and I began to tell him all about my life.

He then injected me with some more of the alien poison and I started to feel light-headed. He made me walk the plank again but I got dizzy and fell off. I started to get annoyed and tried to push the alien out of the way but I fell over. I felt sick and I tried to tell him but the words came out wrong. Everything seemed blurry and the room started to move about. I slid down the wall and tried to find something to hold onto. By now the spaceship seemed to be spinning. Suddenly I was sick all down the front of my shirt. My legs and arms felt heavy and I couldn't stand up. I was sick again. My stomach and throat hurt and I couldn't think straight. The alien just watched. I knew he was trying to kill me. I tried to shout but it came out as a grunt. By now I could hardly move. I put my face on the cold floor and waited to die.

I woke up at home. I was cold, aching and covered in sick. I had a thumping headache and my mouth tasted disgusting. I had no idea how I'd got back home. I felt ill all day. Eventually I had a shower and something to eat but it made me feel sick again. The next day I felt a bit better. That alien tried to kill me.

Activity sheet – Problems with alcohol

Alien report

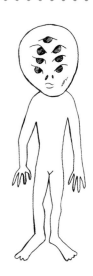

Read the Resource sheet, 'Alien abduction'.

The poison that the alien injected into Jake was alcohol. He was doing an experiment to find out about the short-term effects of alcohol on the human body. The chart below is the alien's observation sheet of Jake.

 Read Jake's account carefully and complete the sheet for the alien.

Observation sheet – short-term effects of alcohol		
	Physical effects	**Mental effects**
After first dose	Relaxed	Seemed quite happy
After second dose		
After third dose		
Following day		

Not everyone reacts in exactly the same way to alcohol, and the aliens will have to carry out many more experiments to find out how alcohol affects humans... so look out!

The human body

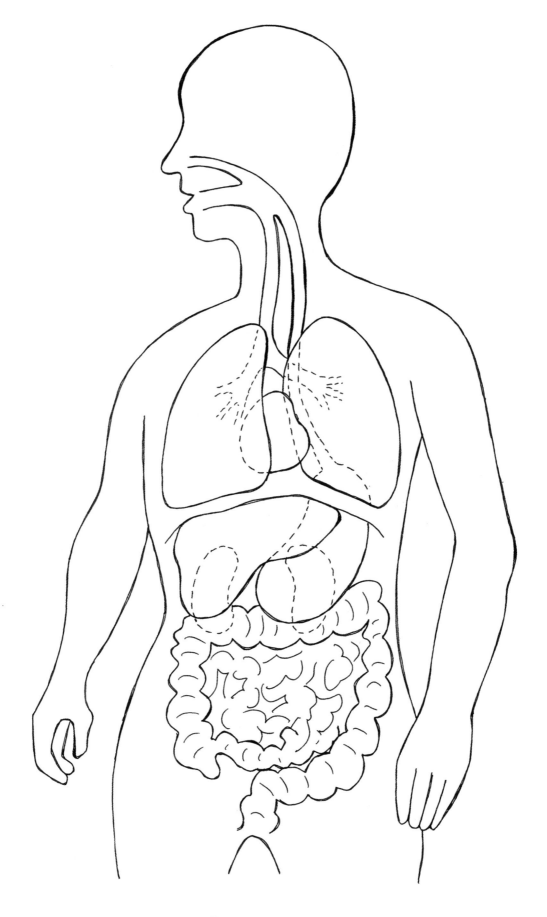

Drugs

Activity sheet – Problems with alcohol

Alcohol in the long term

Drinking too much for many years can have terrible effects on the body. All of the conditions below are more likely to occur in someone who drinks too much alcohol.

☞ Draw an outline of the human body, or alternatively use the template on the Resource sheet, 'The human body'. Label it with the medical conditions listed below to show the damage that drinking too much can do. Use arrows to show which parts of the body are affected.

Cirrhosis of the liver	Mouth cancer	Memory loss
Heart disease	Stroke	Raised blood pressure
Throat cancer	Weight gain	Shrunken genitals
Red veins on face	Diabetes	Lower fertility
Enlarged breasts in men	Breast cancer	Pancreatitis
Interrupted sleep	Anxiety and depression	Liver cancer
Bulbous red nose	Increased risk of suicide	

Activity sheet – Problems with alcohol

Georgina's story

I think my mum drinks too much. She works in a bank and is quite stressed when she gets home, so she usually has a glass of wine when she gets in. Then she'll have another glass while she is cooking and another one when we eat. Sometimes she has one more when we're watching telly. Usually she drinks most of a bottle and sometimes she drinks the whole bottle. She doesn't seem to be drunk but I know it's way over the recommended daily amount. She goes out with her friends about once a month and then she really drinks. She comes home drunk and once I heard her being sick. The next day she had a hangover but she just laughed it off and said I didn't need to worry. I do worry though.

According to NHS guidelines, Georgina's mum is a heavy drinker. Yet, many people regularly drink this amount or more. What are the dangers if Georgina's mum continues to drink like this? Is there anything Georgina can do or is it none of her business?

☞ On a separate sheet of paper, write a letter to Georgina suggesting ways she could cope with this situation.

Teacher's notes

Binge drinking

Objectives

- To understand the term 'binge drinking'
- To recognise the dangers of binge drinking
- To learn skills for keeping safe

Prior knowledge

Students require a basic knowledge of the short and long-term effects of alcohol.

Links to the PSHE: Personal Well-being KS3 Programme of Study for England

1.2 Healthy lifestyles
1.3 Risk

Links to the Draft Curriculum for Excellence for Scotland

Health and Well-being: Substance misuse

Links to the Personal and Social Education Framework for Wales

Emotional aspect
Moral aspect
Physical aspect

Links to the Learning for Life and Work: Personal Development requirements for Northern Ireland

Personal health
Self-awareness

Background

In 2005, statistics suggested that 35% of men and 20% of women exceed the recommended limits for safe drinking. This figure is even higher for young people between the ages of 16 and 24. Government guidelines suggest a maximum of between two to three units a day for women and three to four units for men. Since a large glass of wine contains about 3.5 units it is easy to see how allowances can be exceeded.

The term 'binge drinking' has no clear definition and its usage has changed recently. The British Medical Association uses the term to refer to a period of usually two days or more where the drinker becomes repeatedly intoxicated and gives up other activities in order to continue drinking. In popular culture, however, the term 'binge drinking' refers to the practice of going out and getting drunk, typically in an evening. It is often associated with drinking in groups. It is this more popular meaning of the term which we are referring to in this unit.

Starter activity

Ask students what affects how much a person can drink before they begin to feel the effects. Collate a list on the board. This could include age, height and weight, gender, drinking habits, how much you've eaten, how much you drink, what you drink, how quickly you drink, your emotions and individual differences between people.

Resource sheets and Activity sheets

The guidelines for safe drinking can be very confusing. It is commonly said that two units is a pint of beer or a glass of wine but this varies widely depending on the particular drink. The Activity sheet, 'How much is too much?', can be used as an introduction to the idea that alcohol is measured in units and that the amount of alcohol varies in different drinks. The Activity sheet, 'Why do people binge drink?' and the Resource sheet, 'What are the dangers?', can be used together to look at the ups and downs of binge drinking. It is important to acknowledge that many people enjoy drinking and that it is a part of our culture before looking at the dangers.

The Activity sheet, 'The last good night', is based on a true story and students may well be aware of other stories involving deaths after drinking. In addition to deaths by accidents, approximately 15 young people die each year as a result of alcohol poisoning.

The Activity sheet, 'What would you do if… ?', could be used as a basis for discussion, or you could ask students to role play the situations. You will have to establish firm guidelines about acting drunk. The situations do not necessarily have easy answers. For example, if the girl in the second scenario refuses to get in the car she could find herself alone in town at night.

Plenary

Give students five minutes to put together a radio advert aimed at discouraging binge drinking. Share some of the ideas as a class.

Activity sheet – Binge drinking

How much is too much?

Alcohol is measured in units but different drinks contain different amounts, so it can be very difficult to work out how many units there are in a drink. The recommended guidelines for adults are as follows:

	Maximum units for a week	Maximum units in any one day
Men	21	3 to 4
Women	14	2 to 3

Many people in the UK regularly drink more than the recommended limit. The pictures below give a rough idea of the amount of alcohol in different drinks.

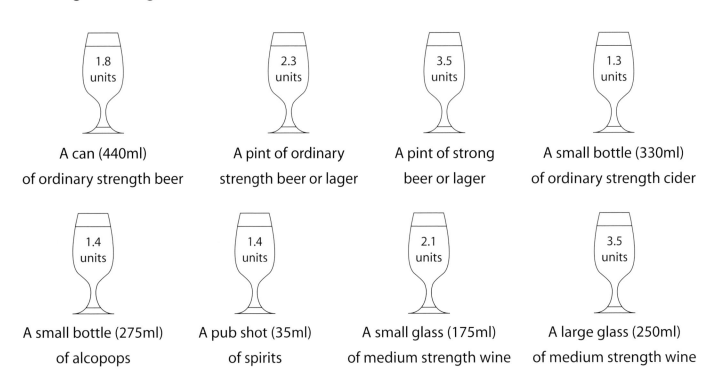

| 1.8 units | 2.3 units | 3.5 units | 1.3 units |
| A can (440ml) of ordinary strength beer | A pint of ordinary strength beer or lager | A pint of strong beer or lager | A small bottle (330ml) of ordinary strength cider |

| 1.4 units | 1.4 units | 2.1 units | 3.5 units |
| A small bottle (275ml) of alcopops | A pub shot (35ml) of spirits | A small glass (175ml) of medium strength wine | A large glass (250ml) of medium strength wine |

☞ 1 Caroline has a small glass of wine each evening on Monday to Friday. She has a pint of ordinary strength beer on Saturday and a gin and tonic on Sunday. Discuss with a partner if she is within her recommended limit.

☞ 2 Design a poster giving information to adults about safe drinking limits.

Activity sheet – Binge drinking

Why do people binge drink?

The phrase 'binge drinking' is often used in the media but it doesn't have a clear meaning. The government describes it as 'drinking excessive amounts of alcohol within a limited period.' Essentially, getting drunk is binge drinking.

Some people can feel drunk on just a few drinks; others can drink a bit more before they feel the effects. This depends partly on your size, gender and drinking habits. Binge drinking is often something people do with others on a night out.

Read Clara and Josh's comments below.

I look forward to Saturday nights out with my friends. Drinking helps me relax and feel like I fit in. We have a laugh and I do and say stuff I wouldn't have the nerve to do normally. I don't usually drink too much, although I am sick sometimes. I usually feel rough the next day.

All my mates drink so I'd look a right idiot if I didn't join in. We don't look for trouble but when you've had a drink you do get a bit rowdy. I've got into a few fights and once a mate of mine fell over and broke his wrist, but that's the price you pay for a good night out.

☞ 1 On a separate sheet of paper, list the reasons why people binge drink. Clara and Josh's comments should give you some ideas to get started.

☞ 2 Now look at the Resource sheet, 'What are the dangers?'. On a separate sheet of paper, list the dangers of binge drinking, using ideas from the Resource sheet and from Josh and Clara's comments.

☞ 3 What advice would you give someone who regularly goes out binge drinking?

What are the dangers?

The last good night

The newspaper article below is based on a true story, although the names have been changed.

Body found

The body of Ben Cheswick was found yesterday in the River Wear about 300 yards from where he was last seen in Durham on Saturday night. Ben was returning home after a night out with friends when he disappeared by the edge of the river. Best friend, Douglas Hardy, said, 'No one saw him fall. We were all walking along, when I realised he wasn't with us any more. At first I wasn't worried. I thought he'd just joined up with another group of lads behind us. When I called for him the next day his mum said he hadn't come home. I just wish I'd seen him. Maybe we could have saved him. No one even looked.'

Police believe Ben probably stumbled into the water by mistake. Detective Inspector Morgan said, 'By all accounts Ben was a nice lad who never caused any trouble. He'd been out for a few beers. The path runs right beside the river and it wouldn't take much for someone to fall in.'

In 2005, about 590 people died in car accidents where the driver had been drinking. Estimates suggest that about 400 people a year die in accidents at home caused by someone who has been drinking. About 10 people a year drown after drinking.

☞ Design a poster warning people about the risk of having an accident if you drink. Include advice for keeping safe when you are out with friends.

Activity sheet – Binge drinking

What would you do if... ?

No one wants to be the odd one out but sometimes going along with your friends can put you at risk.

☞ Discuss each of the following situations with a partner. What would you do in each case? Be honest but try to find a solution which would keep everyone safe.

Your mate has already had loads to drink. You know she'll be sick if she keeps going.

You have been offered a lift home by two boys you know and like, but you suspect that the driver has been drinking. Both your friends are getting in the car.

Your mates are teasing you because you can't drink as much as they can. They have bought you another pint but you know you've had enough.

On the way home you realise one of your group is missing. Your other friends say he'll be fine and tell you to stop worrying.

Teacher's notes

Up in smoke

Objectives

- To understand the dangers of smoking
- To think about how smoking might affect in the future
- To understand that smoking is addictive

Prior knowledge

Students require a basic knowledge of some of the medical problems that can be caused by smoking.

Links to the PSHE: Personal Well-being KS3 Programme of Study for England

1.2 Healthy lifestyles
1.3 Risk

Links to the Draft Curriculum for Excellence for Scotland

Health and Well-being: Substance misuse

Links to the Personal and Social Education Framework for Wales

Emotional aspect
Moral aspect
Physical aspect

Links to the Learning for Life and Work: Personal Development requirements for Northern Ireland

Personal health
Self-awareness

Background

Although girls are more likely to start smoking than boys, of those who do smoke, boys tend to smoke more than girls. More people are quitting smoking than ever before, and this is thought to be a result of government campaigns along with new laws which prohibit smoking in enclosed public spaces. Although it is still too early to assess the impact of the smoking restrictions in the UK, studies of New York and Ireland, where similar smoking restrictions have been in place since 2003 and 2004, have found significant improvements in the pulmonary health of bar workers and a reduction in admissions to hospitals for heart attacks. Eighty per cent of smokers begin smoking before the age of 19, so targeting young people to prevent them from smoking is a priority for the nation's health.

Starter activity

Ask students at what age they can legally buy cigarettes. Many young people still believe it is 16 but in Scotland, England and Wales the age has been 18 since October 2007.

Resource sheets and Activity sheets

By Key Stage 3, most students will have already done work on the physical effects of smoking. The Activity sheet, 'Smoking: what does it do?', can be used as revision or you can read it through and discuss the health risks in more detail.

The Resource sheet, 'It really does happen', can be used in conjunction with the Activity sheet, 'Thinking ahead'. Students could role play the conversation between young and older Sue before writing it down. Encourage them to think about how young 45 actually is by asking them to think of people they know who are that age, including perhaps, their parents.

All of the statements on the Activity sheet, 'A few won't hurt', are true except the second to last one. Inform students they can get help and advice from their GP to give up smoking at any age.

The Activity sheet, 'Changing image', is designed to help students think about the image associated with smoking. Peer pressure can be used here as you will probably have a number of students who secretly, or not so secretly, think that smoking is 'cool'. By encouraging other students to voice their opinions that smoking is unpleasant, dangerous and not 'cool', (or whatever word they are currently using to mean unfashionable!), you may influence how the smokers of the group feel and think about smoking. Anti-smoking poems can be written for homework and making a display of them could be a good end of term project.

Plenary

Ask students if they know anyone who has successfully given up smoking. End the lesson on a positive note by sharing success stories and strategies which worked for their relatives and friends.

Activity sheet – Up in smoke

Smoking: what does it do?

You have probably had many lessons on the effects of smoking but how much have you remembered? Test yourself by filling in the gaps using the words from the box underneath.

Every year, _____ of people around the world die from diseases caused by smoking. _____ the people who smoke for most of their adult life will die from a smoking related disease. Many of these will die before they reach _____ age. Smoking can lead to _____ attacks, _____, _____ and other diseases. It affects the _____ vessels and some smokers end up having legs or arms _____. Many smoking-related diseases are long and slow. Emphysema is an illness that slowly rots away your _____ making it more and more difficult to breathe. Some smokers have to carry _____ cylinders with them. Cigarettes contain over 4000 _____. Many of them are _____ and at least 43 are known to cause cancer.

Missing words:

strokes   poisonous   thousands

blood   cancer   chemicals

heart   lungs

amputated   half

retirement   oxygen

Drugs

It really does happen

I knew smoking was bad for me but I'm only 45 and I still thought there was plenty of time. My daughter was pregnant and I was looking forward to being a young, active granny who could do lots of things with her grandchild. Then, one evening, I started getting pains across my chest and up my arm. My husband called an ambulance and I was rushed into hospital. It was a heart attack. The doctor said it was almost certainly caused by the fact that I was a smoker. While I was in hospital, another lady had been brought in. She had emphysema caused by smoking and she could hardly breathe. Her family took her home but she had a tube up her nose attached to an oxygen cylinder. I thought she was about 70 but the nurse said she was only 63. The nurse said, 'That will be you if you don't give up smoking. That's if you live that long.' That really frightened me and I decided to give up. It was still hard though. I went to my local doctor and he gave me patches which helped. I still get cravings but when I look at my family I remember that other woman in the hospital and I think, 'I don't want to put my family through that.'

Activity sheet – Up in smoke

Thinking ahead

When you are young, it can be hard to imagine what you will think and feel when you are older. Read Sue's story on the Resource sheet, 'It really does happen'.

Sue started smoking when she was 15. If Sue, aged 45, could go back in time and talk to herself when she was 15, what do you think she would say?

☞ Below are some of the things 15-year-old Sue might say. On a separate sheet of paper, write what 45-year-old Sue might say to each statement if she could talk to her younger self.

I know smoking is bad for me but I'll give up when I'm older.

I don't really care what happens to me when I'm old. I just want to have fun now.

I might die young anyway. Plenty of other things besides smoking can kill you.

All my friends smoke and I want to be like them.

I don't care if I die young. I don't want to be old anyway.

Activity sheet – Up in smoke

A few won't hurt

Some people think that if they only smoke a small amount it won't do them any harm but smoking is addictive, which means that once you start, it can become very difficult to stop.

☞ 1 Take a look at the statements below. How many do you think are true? Place a tick in the appropriate column if you think a statement is true and a cross in the other if you think it is false.

	True	False
The main chemical which is addictive in cigarettes is nicotine.		
Young people are more likely to become addicted to nicotine than older people.		
You can become addicted after smoking just a few cigarettes.		
Cigarettes affect your brain, making you feel more relaxed.		
After a while, you need to smoke more to get the same effects.		
People who are addicted often claim that they are not.		
80% of smokers began smoking before they were 19.		
Your doctor can give you advice and help to give up smoking.		
You cannot get help to give up smoking if you are under 18.		
Nicotine patches and gum can help you give up smoking.		

☞ 2 Design a poster aimed at persuading young people either to give up smoking or not to start in the first place.

Changing image

Smoking was once seen as glamorous but now that we know smoking kills people most of us see it very differently.

☞ 1 Circle the words below which *you* associate with smoking.

glamorous	smelly	dangerous	sexy
exciting	daring	fun	stupid
relaxing	fashionable	grown-up	pointless
anti-social	selfish	safe	risky	deadly
wasteful	sad	expensive	friendly

Oscar, aged 14, wrote the following poem about smoking:

Smoking

Smelly and mindless

Makes you feel sick

Only losers do it

Keen to look big

Imagine their lungs!

Nicotine drenched

Gonna die early. Losers.

☞ 2 Write your own poem describing what you think of smoking. You could use the letters from the word smoking, like Oscar, or you could use some of the words you circled above.

Drugs

Teacher's notes

Why do young people smoke?

Objectives

- To consider the factors which influence young people's decisions to smoke
- To develop strategies to deal with peer pressure

Prior knowledge

Students require a basic knowledge of some of the health effects of smoking.

Links to the PSHE: Personal Well-being KS3 Programme of Study for England

1.2   Healthy lifestyles
1.3   Risk

Links to the Draft Curriculum for Excellence for Scotland

Health and Well-being: Substance misuse

Links to the Personal and Social Education Framework for Wales

Emotional aspect
Moral aspect
Physical aspect

Links to the Learning for Life and Work: Personal Development requirements for Northern Ireland

Personal health
Self-awareness

Background

According to government surveys, the number of young people smoking between the ages of 11 and 15 remained fairly static between 2003 and 2006. The 2006 survey found that 9% of people in this age group were regular smokers, with girls more likely to be smokers than boys. As one would expect, older children are more likely to smoke than young children. Only 1% of eleven year olds reported smoking within the last week but amongst 15 year olds this rose to 20%.

Starter activity

Compile a list of things that you can legally do but which are dangerous, for example, sports, driving, smoking. Why do people do dangerous things? In which cases do the benefits outweigh the risks?

Resource sheets and Activity sheets

The Resource sheets, 'Jack's story' and 'Meera's story', can be used independently as discussion starters or they can be used together to carry out the activities on the Activity sheet, 'Are they right?'. You may need to have a class discussion to tease out the less obvious reasons why the two young people smoke. For example, Meera may have lost some self-confidence when she moved and found she couldn't make friends easily.

The Activity sheet, 'Why *don't* young people smoke?', focuses on the fact that many young people make the positive choice not to smoke. Students could write the TV scripts or, if you have the time, you could do a whole-class TV show in the style of the Oprah Winfrey/Trisha shows. Two students could act the role of young people who want to give up smoking. A presenter could interview them and then interview an expert who gives reasons not to smoke. The rest of the class can then play the role of the audience who are invited to add their comments. You or your most confident student will need to take the role of the presenter.

The Activity sheet, 'No friend of mine', aims to show that the group's response will depend very much on the boy's answer. If he gives in and agrees to smoke, the others in the group will probably keep quiet but, if he refuses, the others may find the courage to back him. Students could trace the picture and show the next scene, where the characters think and say different things. The speech bubbles could be changed to thought bubbles and vice versa. Alternatively, students could role play the scene.

Plenary

If students were asked to advise the government on ways to reduce smoking in young people, what one strategy would they recommend as the most effective method of cutting smoking?

Jack's story

My mum and my stepdad both smoke. I remember mum giving me her fag to hold once when she was trying to find something in her bag and I tried to take a puff. She went ballistic and shouted at me. I was only about five. They've always nagged at me not to smoke which I think is hypocritical. Last year, when I kept getting into trouble at school, they threatened to ground me but I went out anyway. I used to go to the rec with some mates. One of them got hold of a packet of fags and we all smoked them. I didn't like it at first but I kept doing it. It made me laugh to think how mad my mum would be if she found out. Now most of my mates smoke. It's something to do and I don't really care about the future. I'll give up when I'm older.

Drugs

Resource sheet – Why do young people smoke?

Meera's story

When I started at my new school it was really difficult to make friends. There were the geeky girls, the girls who thought they were 'it' and the skanky lot that hang about the toilet block. I didn't seem to fit in anywhere. Then I started talking to Jen and she introduced me to some of her friends. They all hang about up the top of the field and meet up most weekends. They like the same music as me and they're into clothes but not in a fashion victim way. They all work hard at school, too, which is good because I want to do well. But they all smoke so I thought, well, why not? I don't inhale much so I don't think it will do me too much harm. To be honest, I think it makes us look older. We're not like the lot in the toilet block who rush off to light up and gossip about it and feel big. We just smoke when we feel like it. It's no big deal. I did ask Jen once why she started smoking and she said it helps keep her weight down. That seems like a pretty good reason to me – after all, being overweight is a health risk too.

Drugs

Activity sheet – Why do young people smoke?

Are they right?

Jack and Meera both think they will not harm their health because they don't smoke or inhale much. Are they right?

☞ 1 On the Resource sheets, 'Jack's story' and 'Meera's story' they both tell us some reasons why they smoke. Using the two Resource sheets and any of your own ideas, fill in the chart below with the reasons that Jack and Meera smoke.

Jack's reasons	Meera's reasons

Now look at the reasons on your chart. Do you think they are good reasons to smoke? What would you say to Jack or Meera if they gave those reasons for smoking?

☞ 2 Write a letter to either Jack or Meera persuading them to give up smoking. You will need to discuss their reasons for smoking and say why they might be wrong.

Drugs

Why *don't* young people smoke?

Some people make the choice to smoke. But some people make the choice not to smoke.
Read the comments below.

My nan died when she was only 63 because she smoked for nearly 50 years.

My boyfriend smoked. His clothes smelled and it was like kissing an ashtray.

I wouldn't waste my money on fags. I'd much rather spend it on music and going out.

In our school, it tends to be the thicker kids who smoke.

Every time my uncle lights up he tells me never to start because it's so difficult to give up.

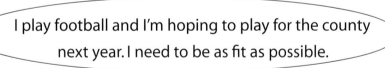

I play football and I'm hoping to play for the county next year. I need to be as fit as possible.

You can't smoke in pubs and restaurants now so if you want one you have to go outside. You miss out on the conversation and get freezing cold or wet sometimes.

Smoking is going out of fashion. Loads of older people do it but more young people are choosing not to.

Smoking kills you!

☞ Role play or write a script for a TV programme where you interview young people who have chosen not to smoke. Try to get a variety of reasons.

No friend of mine

Peer pressure works both ways. Look at the picture below.

☞ Fill in the empty speech bubble with an answer the boy might give. Compare your idea with those of other people. On a separate sheet of paper, draw the next scene showing what the others might say and think after the boy has spoken. You could also role play some of the scenes.

Drugs

Teacher's notes

Class A, B or C?

Objectives

- To understand that drugs are classified as either class A, B or C
- To gain some knowledge about the law relating to class A, B and C drugs
- To consider the dangers of drug taking

Prior knowledge

It would be useful if students had some knowledge of illegal drugs, including their street names. The unit 'A safer lifestyle: avoiding illegal drugs' in the *PSHE Specials! Healthy lifestyles* would be a useful introduction to this topic.

Links to the PSHE: Personal Well-being KS3 Programme of Study for England

1.2 Healthy lifestyles
1.3 Risk

Links to the Draft Curriculum for Excellence for Scotland

Health and Well-being: Substance misuse

Links to the Personal and Social Education Framework for Wales

Emotional aspect
Moral aspect
Physical aspect

Links to the Learning for Life and Work: Personal Development requirements for Northern Ireland

Personal Health
Self-awareness

Background

According to a government survey in 2006, 9% of young people aged 11 to 15 reported using drugs in the previous month. Seventeen per cent had taken drugs in the last year. As with smoking, this varied with age, with 29% of 15 year olds reporting using drugs within the last year. Drug usage between boys and girls was broadly similar. Children who have truanted or been excluded from school were more likely to have used drugs. Only 1% of students who had never truanted or been excluded from school had used a class A drug. This figure rose to 14% among children who had truanted or been excluded.

Starter activity

Ask students if they would ride a bike on a busy road. Would they ride it one handed? Would they ride it with their eyes shut? Would they ride it on the wrong side of the road with their eyes shut? All of these are risky behaviours but they carry different degrees of risk. Talk about how we balance risk. Why would someone want to do something that was risky? How does this relate to drug taking?

Resource sheets and Activity sheets

Introduce the Activity sheet, 'What's the difference?', by talking about different degrees of risk. All drug taking is risky but drugs are classified according to the degree of dangers involved. Students can then carry out the exercises on the sheet. The maximum prison sentences for drug-related crimes are as follows: Class A – possession: 7 years, supply: life. Class B – possession: 5 years, supply: 14. Class C – possession: 2 years, supply: 14. In all cases judges can impose unlimited fines.

The Activity sheet, 'A, B or C?', helps students classify commonly used drugs. You could ask them to write their answers in pencil before going through the list with the class. Classifications are currently (April 2007) as follows:

Class A drugs: Ecstasy, LSD, Heroin, Cocaine, crack, raw magic mushrooms, dried or cooked magic mushrooms, crystal meth, amphetamines (speed) prepared for injection.

Class B drugs: Amphetamines (speed), Methylphenidate (Ritalin), Pholcodine (found in cough medicines)

Class C drugs: Cannabis, tranquilisers, Gamma hydroxybutyrate (GHB), ketamine.

Cannabis was moved from class B to class C in 2004 but it is possible that it will be reclassified again. In the past, magic mushrooms were only classed as illegal if they were prepared in some way, for example, dried or cooked. This changed in July 2005 and possessing or supplying magic mushrooms in any state, including raw, is now illegal. They are a class A drug.

The Resource sheet, 'Cannabis and me', can be used with the Activity sheet, 'What harm does it do?', to look at the health risks associated with cannabis. The Activity sheet, 'Why class A?', then focuses on the ultimate danger, such as the risk of death from drug taking.

Plenary

Class A drugs are seen as being more dangerous than class C drugs. Does this mean that class C drugs are not dangerous? Discuss this with the students.

Activity sheet – Class A, B or C?

What's the difference?

☞ 1 Complete the information below using the words from the box underneath.

In British law, drugs are _____ as either class A, B or C. In general, the most

_____ drugs and the drugs which are most _____ are class A drugs.

When someone is found _____ of a drug-related crime, their punishment will

depend on the class of the drug that was involved. _____ decide on the

punishment, which can be a prison sentence, a fine or _____.

harmful	guilty	both	classified	judges	addictive

☞ 2 Match the crimes below to the maximum penalties a judge can give. Remember,
the penalties are harsher for class A drugs and harsher for supplying than for
possessing.

Crimes	Maximum penalties
Possession of class A drug	5 years in prison and/or unlimited fine
Supplying class A drug	14 years in prison and/or unlimited fine
Possession of class B drug	14 years in prison and/or unlimited fine
Supplying class B drug	7 years in prison and/or unlimited fine
Possession of class C drug	Life in prison and/or unlimited fine
Supplying class C drug	2 years in prison and/or unlimited fine

☞ 3 Do you think the penalties are too harsh, too soft or about right? Explain your
answers on a separate sheet of paper.

Activity sheet – Class A, B or C?

A, B or C?

Illegal drugs are classified as being class A, B or C. Recently cannabis and raw magic mushrooms have both been reclassified.

☞ 1 Look at the list of drugs below. Label each one A, B or C to show which class you think it is in.

LSD ☐   Ecstasy ☐

Amphetamines aka Speed ☐   Pholcodine (found in cough medicines) ☐

Gamma Hydroxybutyrate (GHB) ☐   Crack ☐

Cocaine ☐   Raw Magic Mushrooms ☐

Tranquillisers ☐   Amphetamines (Speed) prepared for injection ☐

Ketamine ☐
                                                       Methylphenidate (Ritalin) ☐
Dried or cooked Magic Mushrooms ☐
                                                       Heroin ☐
Crystal Meth ☐
                                                       Cannabis ☐

☞ 2 Design a poster showing which drugs are class A, B or C. You could include street names, pictures and information about the penalties for possessing or supplying drugs.

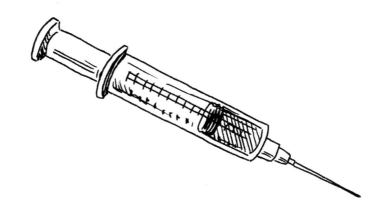

Cannabis and me

I'm Dean and I started smoking pot when I was about 14. Me and some mates would smoke it on a Saturday night. It helped me relax and sometimes we'd talk loads and laugh till we couldn't stop. When I was doing my GCSE's I started smoking it more. I worked hard and I felt like I deserved a treat.

Then I went to college, and later university, where I smoked most days. It didn't interfere with my studies and I did well. I thought it was a good way to unwind. I took a year out and got a job in Canada. I didn't know any dealers and I soon found I couldn't relax without cannabis. After a few weeks I chucked my job. I said it was because it was boring but I know now it was because I wanted to go somewhere where I could get more weed.

I spent the next year doing nothing much and smoking more and more. Then I started to get paranoid. I was living in a shared flat and I was convinced that the other guys were out to get me. I fitted a lock to my door and at night I would lay awake because I thought I could hear them trying to unscrew the hinges on my door.

I was lucky. I told someone about it and she recognised the signs and made me go to the doctor. He sent me to a drug counselling group and eventually I kicked the habit. I still get paranoid but I know now it's the effect of the drug. Since then I've met other cannabis users. I know one guy who is schizophrenic. Evidence suggests that using cannabis can trigger mental illnesses including schizophrenia. Smoking cannabis also increases your risk of lung cancer. Anyone who says it's harmless is a fool!

Activity sheet – Class A, B or C?

What harm does it do?

☞ 1 Read the Resource sheet, 'Cannabis and me'. Write two lists showing the short-term effects and long-term effects of using cannabis, according to Dean.

Short-term effects	Possible long-term effects

☞ 2 Read the comment below. Use the speech bubble to write down the answer that Dean might give.

Cannabis doesn't do any harm. People don't get aggressive like they sometimes do with alcohol and it won't kill you like some other drugs might. It helps you to relax – that's a good thing, right?

☞ 3 Cannabis was moved from a class B drug to a class C drug in 2004 but the government is considering moving it back to class B. What class do you think cannabis should be in? Give reasons for your answer.

Activity sheet – Class A, B or C?

Why class A?

Class A drugs are dangerous. They are often highly addictive and carry huge health risks. Read the news stories below. They are all based on true stories.

Rogue ecstasy kills three

Three people died following a rave in London on Saturday. All three had taken ecstasy and it is now thought that the tablets contained a number of other substances.

Heroine continues to kill

Government statistics show that 713 people died in 2006 in heroin-related deaths.

Mother campaigns after son's death

A woman from Birmingham is campaigning to raise awareness about the dangers of cocaine after her 22-year-old son died. Doctors confirmed that he had a heart attack as a result of taking cocaine.

Sister commits suicide

19 year old Genna Michaels committed suicide yesterday, three months after the death of her 16-year-old sister Morgan. Morgan died of a drugs overdose at a party in January. Friends say that Genna never got over it.

☞ Last year, over 2500 people died in the UK as a result of using drugs. On a separate sheet of paper, write a story about someone who dies after using drugs. You could be a friend or relative of the person, or you could even be the person who dies. Use the news stories above to give you ideas or use your own ideas.

Teacher's notes

Drugs and crime

Objectives

- To gain an understanding of drug-related laws
- To consider the link between drug taking and crime
- To explore attitudes towards drugs and drug addicts
- To explore ways of protecting themselves from drug-related crime

Prior knowledge

Students require a basic understanding that some drugs are illegal.

Links to the PSHE: Personal Well-being KS3 Programme of Study for England

1.2 Healthy lifestyles
1.3 Risk

Links to the Draft Curriculum for Excellence for Scotland

Health and Well-being: Substance misuse

Links to the Personal and Social Education Framework for Wales

Emotional aspect
Moral aspect
Physical aspect

Links to the Learning for Life and Work: Personal Development requirements for Northern Ireland

Personal health
Self-awareness

Starter activity

What drug-related stories can students remember from TV programmes, including soaps? How realistic do they think these stories are?

Resource sheets and Activity sheets

The Resource sheet, 'All guilty', can be used with the Activity sheet, 'Which charge?'. You will probably need to read through the four boxes, describing the charges, with students to ensure they understand them before they look at the scenarios. The legal term for an illegal drug is 'controlled substance' but the term 'drug' has been used here for simplification.

Students may need help in identifying sources of help for the task on the Activity sheet, 'Getting help'. They could use the Internet, local phone book and any posters you may have around school.

The Activity sheet, 'Drug-related crime', encourages students to think about the links between drug use and crime, as well as about their own attitudes to drug taking and drug addicts. Students could tick the boxes individually, then get together in pairs to compare answers. Encourage them to justify their choices where differences arise. The task on the Activity sheet, 'Don't be a victim', could be set for homework.

Plenary

The penalties for supplying drugs are harsher than the penalties for using drugs. Why is this? Do students think this is right?

Background

There is huge controversy about drug-related crime. Government policy sees reducing drug use as essential in reducing 'acquisition' crimes, for example, burglary, theft and shoplifting. Other organisations think the link is less direct; however, most people agree that crime and drugs are strongly linked. A recent survey discovered that the most frequently cited reason for thefts and burglaries among prisoners who admit to using drugs, was 'needing to pay for a drug habit'.

All guilty

John often smokes cannabis at home. His mum knows and has told him to stop but he carries on. In the end she says that she will ignore it as long as he promises never to smoke it in front of his younger brother.

Kelly buys an ecstasy tablet for the weekend but she is worried that her mum will find it in her room, so she gives it to her friend, Ella, to look after. Ella keeps the tablet till Friday and then gives it back to Kelly.

Amber has found a place where magic mushrooms grow so she picks some. She texts her friend, Fern, and tells her that she will give her some the next day.

Gary doesn't do drugs but he knows someone who deals in amphetamines. He buys some and sells them at a profit in a local club.

Activity sheet – Drugs and crime

Which charge?

☞ Read the Resource sheet, 'All guilty'. Now read the boxes below to find out about the drug-related offences the people in the stories could be charged with. Fill in the chart at the bottom of the page to show which charge each person could face.

Possession of drugs – this means you have a drug on you. This can include in your pocket or bag.

Possession of drugs with intent to supply – you have drugs on you and police can prove that you intend to give or sell them to someone else.

Supplying or offering to supply drugs – you have sold or given drugs to someone, or offered to. This includes sharing drugs with a mate, giving them back drugs they asked you to look after or handing drugs over in any other way, even if no money is involved. You have still committed this offence even if the person you offer the drugs to says no.

Allowing your premises to be used for drug offences – this means allowing someone to use or supply drugs in a building you own, rent or manage. It could be a house, flat, shop, club or any other building. If you know about the drug use that counts as 'allowing' it, even if you have told the person to stop and they continue without your permission.

Person	Charge
John	
John's mum	
Kelly	
Ella	
Amber	
Gary	

Activity sheet – Drugs and crime

Getting help

Aidan has just been arrested for burglary. Read his statement.

I used to smoke dope at school. I knew it was bad for you but it made me feel good. When I left school, I got a job and started going out at the weekends. That's when I began using crack. It felt great but then I found I couldn't get through the day without it. I managed to stop for a bit but then I split up with my girlfriend and started doing crack again. This time I was doing more than ever and I just couldn't afford it. One day, I was in a shop looking at some games and before I knew it I'd put one in my pocket. I sold it to a mate. After that I did quite a bit of shoplifting and I met a bloke on the market who could flog the stuff for me. Then, last summer, when I was walking home, I saw a house with a back window open. There was no one about so I just climbed in and took some stuff. After that, I started going out most weekends and nicking stuff. I wish I could stop doing crack. It's ruining my life. I need help.

☞ 1 Aidan says he needs help. Make a list of all the places and people he could go to get help with his addiction.

Eventually, Aidan manages to give up crack and he gets his life back on track. He decides to go into schools to talk to young people about drug abuse and where it can lead.

☞ 2 Write the speech that Aidan might give to a group of 14 year olds about his life and what he has learned.

Drugs

Drug-related crime

There is a strong link between drug taking and other crimes. Eighty per cent of burglaries are thought to be drug-related and 55% of prisoners who admitted using drugs said their offences were linked to their drug usage. Why do you think there is such a strong link between drug taking and crime?

☞ 1 Read the statements below and, for each one, tick one of the boxes to show whether you 'strongly agree', 'agree', 'disagree' or 'strongly disagree'.

Statement	Strongly agree	Agree	Disagree	Strongly disagree
Drug addicts need to steal to pay for their drugs.				
If you take drugs you are more likely to commit other crimes.				
Drug addicts can't help what they do.				
People who take drugs are bad, so are more likely to commit crimes.				
If a drug addict agrees to get treatment they should not have to go to jail.				
If all drugs were legal, like cigarettes, then people wouldn't commit crimes to get them.				
Some people take drugs without doing any harm to anyone else.				
Drug addicts who steal should be helped, not punished.				

☞ 2 Compare your answers with others in your class. Discuss any differences.

Don't be a victim

Even if you never knowingly take illegal drugs, you can end up a victim of drug-related crime. Read the stories below.

Keira left her drink on the table while she played darts. Someone put Rohypnol in it. She became confused and felt very drunk. A man offered to help her but instead he took her to a hotel and raped her.

Gareth was walking home late one night when he was mugged. The gang who mugged him used the money to buy amphetamines.

Jodie was out with her friends when she was hit by a car. The driver had been smoking cannabis.

Oliver had some space in his suitcase so he let his friend pack some things in it on their way back from Amsterdam. The 'things' turned out to be drugs hidden in a sock. The police don't believe that Oliver didn't know.

You can't always keep out of trouble but there are a lot of things you can do to help keep yourself safe.

☞ Design a poster or leaflet for young people with ideas on keeping safe and avoiding becoming a victim of drug-related crime.

Teacher's notes

Drugs and driving

Objectives

- To understand the dangers of drugs and driving
- To appreciate that legal drugs can also make driving dangerous

Prior knowledge

Students require no prior knowledge for this unit.

Links to the PSHE: Personal Well-being KS3 Programme of Study for England

1.2   Healthy lifestyles
1.3   Risk

Links to the Draft Curriculum for Excellence for Scotland

Health and Well-being: Substance misuse

Links to the Personal and Social Education Framework for Wales

Emotional aspect
Moral aspect
Physical aspect

Links to the Learning for Life and Work: Personal Development requirements for Northern Ireland

Personal health
Self-awareness

Background

Research shows that 22% of people killed in road traffic accidents have illegal drugs in their blood stream. The Transport Research Laboratory carried out tests on drivers after they had smoked a joint and found that at 66mph, stopping distances increased by 15% and, in a slalom test, the amount of cones knocked over increased by 30%. There is also concern that some legal drugs can affect a person's ability to drive, and little research has been done into the effects of combining different drugs or combining drugs with alcohol, although it is known that alcohol can alter or intensify the way drugs react on a body. There are theories which say that some drugs (particularly amphetamines) improve someone's ability to drive. There is no evidence to support this theory.

Starter activity

Play hangman with the phrase 'Don't drink and drive'. Once students have guessed it talk about why this is such a well-known phrase. Are the dangers of drugs and driving equally well known?

Resource sheets and Activity sheets

Students could work in small groups to complete the chart on the Activity sheet, 'How does it affect your driving?'.

Students will need the Resource sheet, 'Liam's ride home', to complete the work on the Activity sheet, 'Drugs and driving: the facts'. Of the true or false statements, the first two are true. The others are false as the figures have been halved in each case. The true figures are 22%, 80% and 800,000 respectively.

The Activity sheets, 'Medicines and driving' and 'Fit to drive?', focus on the effects of legal drugs. There are many things which, although not illegal, may have affected Graham's ability to react quickly. You should highlight things like feeling ill, being tired, taking more than one medicine and combining medicines with alcohol. You could also point out that speed limits are a maximum and that a 30mph limit doesn't mean it is necessarily safe to drive at that speed, depending on the road conditions.

Plenary

'Don't drink and drive' is a well-known anti-drink driving slogan. Challenge students to come up with an equally snappy anti-drugs and driving slogan.

Activity sheet – Drugs and driving

How does it affect your driving?

☞ Look at the chart below, which shows the effects of some drugs. Complete the chart showing why it would be dangerous to drive if you had taken each of these drugs. The first one has been done for you.

Drug	Effects	Why this makes you unfit to drive
alcohol	Slows reactions. Can make you feel relaxed and sleepy or aggressive. Can blur vision.	You will be too slow to react to things. You can't concentrate. You may drive aggressively. You may not be able to see the road clearly.
cannabis	Slows reactions. You feel relaxed and may feel there is nothing to worry about. Can affect your vision or make you feel sleepy.	
cocaine	You feel wide awake and super-confident. It can affect how you see things or judge speed and distances. Afterwards, you may feel low, sleepy or miserable.	
LSD	You may see things that are not there. Things appear to speed up or slow down. Co-ordination skills are affected, vision can be blurred and you may feel as if you are not really there. Later, you may experience flashbacks without warning.	
ecstasy	You feel full of energy, super-confident and talkative. Things seem clearer and brighter. Your concentration is affected. You may get panic attacks or feel confused.	
Ampheta-mine (Speed)	You feel wide awake, excited and chatty. Your co-ordination and sense of speed and timing are affected. You may get panic attacks. Later, you can feel irritable and depressed.	

Drugs

Liam's ride home

I'd been out clubbing with some friends. We had a fantastic time and I felt great but the guy who was supposed to be giving me a lift home had been drinking, so I didn't want to get in his car. I asked around and Glen offered me a lift instead. He said he hadn't been drinking but he had taken some Speed. He said that Speed made you concentrate and kept you awake so it would help his driving. Someone else told me that Speed was the same stuff they give kids with ADHD to make them concentrate, and that fighter pilots are given Speed when they're flying in Iraq and Afghanistan. They made it sound like Speed would improve Glen's driving.

As soon as we set off I could tell he was driving too fast. He overtook on a corner, came off the road and hit a tree.

My doctor said that drugs used to treat ADHD and for pilots are carefully controlled and measured, whereas Glen had no idea what he was taking. Speed makes you feel confident and willing to take risks, which is fine for a fighter pilot but not so great in a teenage driver. He also said Speed can affect your co-ordination and how you judge speed and distances. I thought I'd be safe with Glen. I'm lucky to be alive.

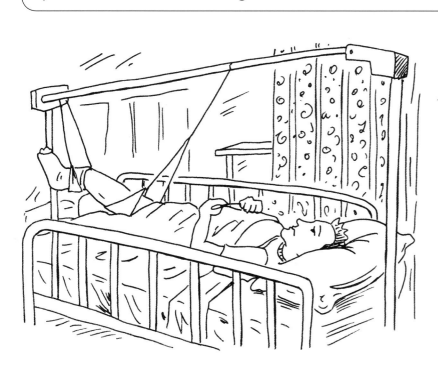

Activity sheet – Drugs and driving

Drugs and driving: the facts

Read the Resource sheet, 'Liam's ride home'. Liam thought he was doing the right thing avoiding a lift from someone who had been drinking but he didn't know about the dangers of drugs and driving. What should he have done?

☞ 1 Now read the statements below and tick the boxes to show whether you think they are true or false. Afterwards, check your answers with the teacher.

		True	False
a	Driving while under the influence of drugs is most common in the 20 to 24 year old age group.	☐	☐
b	Some prescription medicines can make you sleepy or affect your co-ordination.	☐	☐
c	11% of people killed in road accidents have traces of drugs in their blood.	☐	☐
d	In a recent survey in Scotland, 40% of clubbers interviewed said they had driven while under the influence of drugs at some time.	☐	☐
e	Estimates suggest that there are over 400 000 cases in the UK every year of people driving shortly after smoking cannabis.	☐	☐

☞ 2 On a separate sheet of paper, design a leaflet warning people of the dangers of driving and drugs.

Drugs

Medicines and driving

Some prescription or over-the-counter medicines have side effects that may make driving dangerous. The following is a list of side effects which you may find on medicine leaflets. If you have suffered from any of these side effects you should avoid driving.

☞ 1 Find the words which are underlined in the word search below.

Drowsiness

Dizziness or feeling light-headed

Difficulty concentrating

Feeling edgy, angry or aggressive

Feeling sick

Reduced co-ordination

Feeling shaky and unstable

A	C	T	E	N	D	A	U	N	Z	W	M	L	S
D	R	O	W	S	I	N	E	S	S	V	C	Q	N
I	K	M	N	A	N	G	S	I	R	Z	P	Y	E
Z	D	T	K	C	O	R	W	C	P	T	K	A	L
Z	O	R	Y	N	E	Y	D	K	F	A	D	M	B
I	V	G	M	S	W	N	E	Q	H	R	T	V	A
N	D	E	J	T	A	F	T	S	N	D	O	C	T
E	G	K	D	L	F	Z	O	R	V	M	U	W	S
S	X	C	O	O	R	D	I	N	A	T	I	O	N
S	A	K	C	X	B	Y	U	V	F	T	H	Y	U
A	F	D	R	T	L	N	M	V	H	S	I	J	R
L	I	G	H	T	H	E	A	D	E	D	K	N	L
T	P	A	G	G	R	E	S	S	I	V	E	A	G

Drivers should take extra care if they:

- take more than one medicine
- are already feeling ill or tired
- take more than the required dose
- drink alcohol.

☞ 2 On a separate sheet of paper, design a poster warning people of the danger of driving when taking medicines.

Fit to drive?

Read the story below.

Graham had a bad cold. He was awake most of the night coughing. The next day he drove to work feeling terrible. At work he made himself a hot lemon drink using a sachet designed for treating colds and flu. Later, he took some paracetamol for his headache. By lunchtime he felt worse and decided to go home. At home he took some cough medicine and then he had a small whiskey. He decided to drive to the chemist to get some more cough medicine. It was raining. The window in his car steamed up so he wiped it with his sleeve. He was doing 30mph in a 30 zone. Suddenly a young girl stepped out into the road. He hit the brakes but the car skidded straight into her. She died before the ambulance arrived. The police did a breath test on Graham but he was within the legal limit for alcohol.

At the inquest the judge ruled that it had been an accident. Graham is not so sure. At night he lays awake thinking about all the things that happened that day which might have affected his reaction time. No one blames Graham. Except Graham.

☞ 1 Underline all the things that happened that day which could have had an effect on Graham's driving.

☞ 2 Although Graham did not break the law, he made some poor choices. What could he have done differently, which might have meant the accident didn't happen?

Teacher's notes

Parents against drugs

Objectives

- To learn about one of the voluntary organisations tackling drug abuse
- To understand the role of parents in preventing drug abuse

Prior knowledge

Students require a basic knowledge that illegal drugs can be harmful.

Links to the PSHE: Personal Well-being KS3 Programme of Study for England

1.2 Healthy lifestyles
1.3 Risk

Links to the Draft Curriculum for Excellence for Scotland

Health and Well-being: Substance misuse

Links to the Personal and Social Education Framework for Wales

Emotional aspect
Moral aspect
Physical aspect

Links to the Learning for Life and Work: Personal Development requirements for Northern Ireland

Personal health
Self-awareness

Background

Parents Against Drug Abuse (PADA) is a real organisation with a national helpline, local support groups and other services to support parents and families of substance users. There are also a number of other voluntary organisations, which play an important role in providing support for drug users and their families. Many people prefer to seek help from voluntary organisations partly because they know they will be helped by people who have been through similar problems and partly because of a reluctance to involve the authorities. Local authority services are also limited in some areas.

Starter activity

Ask students to guess how many registered charities there are in England and Wales. The answer in 2006 was 169 333. Hold a brief discussion on the role of charities.

Resource sheets and Activity sheets

The Resource sheet, 'Parents Against Drug Abuse (PADA)', should be used with the Activity sheet, 'Parent power'. You could ask students to think of interview questions in pairs, then share ideas and select the best questions for students to answer. Try to encourage questions which will elicit interesting answers rather than simply factual ones. The TV programme could then be scripted or performed as a role play.

The newspaper report on the Activity sheet, 'Keeping teenagers safe', is based on real research carried out by Newcastle University in 2002. You could hold a class discussion on the other factors which might increase the likelihood of drug abuse, before students write their letters.

The rules or guidelines on the Resource sheet, 'How to be a good parent', are adapted from a handbook written by the National Youth Anti-Drug Media Campaign. You could read through the rules with students before giving them the Activity sheet, 'Parenting in action'. The activity on this sheet should provoke discussion about what is and isn't reasonable for parents to do. The last picture, for example, could be seen as a caring parent checking up on a teenager, or could be seen as a nosey parent not trusting their teenager or allowing them privacy. You might want to discuss when it would or would not be acceptable to check up on a child.

Plenary

This unit has been about parents with children who are using drugs but where can children go for help if they are worried about an adult using drugs? Ask students for ideas and compile a list on the board. This might include teachers, another trusted adult, doctors, school counsellors, Childline and any local services.

Parents Against Drug Abuse (PADA)

Why?

In the 1980s, heroin addiction was becoming a problem in many parts of the UK. At the time, there was very little help for people with drug addictions or their families, outside of London.

How did it start?

When Joan Keogh discovered that both her children were using heroin, she went to her local doctor for help. He couldn't offer much but he gave her the names of a number of other parents with the same problem. Joan arranged a meeting in the local hall and 250 people turned up. This was in the Wirral, near Liverpool, in 1984. Parents Against Drug Abuse (PADA) grew from this first meeting.

What did they do then?

PADA campaigned for services to help drug users and their families. Gradually, the government and the local council began providing services.

What do they do now?

PADA still campaign for better services but they also do many other things, including:

- helping set up local support groups for parents across the country
- training volunteers to support parents
- running a national helpline for parents, which receives over 15 000 calls a year
- running one-to-one and family counselling sessions
- offering alternative therapy treatments.

What is their helpline number?

08457 023867

Activity sheet – Parents against drugs

Parent power

Read the Resource sheet, 'Parents Against Drug Abuse (PADA)'.

Shelley phoned PADA last year. Read what she has to say.

> I found some white powder in my son's room. I was terrified. I phoned PADA and they gave me advice on what it might be and how to approach my son. Instead of going mad at him, I talked to him calmly and he admitted he had a problem. He agreed to come to the doctor with me and now he is on a rehab program. Without PADA I think I would have overreacted and just made things worse.

☞ 1 You have been asked to interview one of the organisers of Parents Against Drug Abuse for a TV programme. Use the space below to write a list of questions you might ask. Two have been done for you.

    a   How did Parents Against Drug Abuse start?

    b   Most of the volunteers who work for PADA are parents whose children have had drug problems. Why do you think these people make good support workers?

    c _____

        _____

    d _____

        _____

    e _____

        _____

    f _____

        _____

☞ 2 Now write or perform the script for the TV programme. You could include an interview with Shelley as well.

Keeping teenagers safe

☞ Read the following news report.

Caring mums save kids from drugs

An international study led by Newcastle University found that young people who had a good relationship with their mothers were less likely to develop a drug habit. Researchers questioned almost 4000 youngsters aged 14 to 15, in five different countries, to find out what stopped children from getting involved with drugs.

It seems that children who are supervised and spend quality time with their families are less

likely to turn to drugs. Dr McArdle, who led the research, said 'This study shows that the quality of family life, or rather the lack of it for many young people, is at the core of the drugs problem in Western society.'

☞ 1 Do you agree or disagree that families can affect whether or not young people use drugs? On a separate sheet of paper, write a list of other things which might affect a young person's decision to use drugs.

☞ 2 Write a letter to the newspaper saying either:

- why you think families are so important in preventing drug problems in young people

or

- what you think is more important than families in preventing drug problems in young people.

How to be a good parent

Tune in

Listen to your teenager

Talk about things

Get to know their friends

Take an interest in their hobbies

Spend time with your teenager

Give guidance

Set and/or negotiate rules

Be clear about what you expect

Be clear about consequences if rules are broken

Check that your teenager is doing what they say

Discuss your beliefs, values, hopes and worries

Show respect

Show respect to your teenager

Allow them some privacy

Trust them where possible

Listen to their opinions

Don't make fun of their clothes, friends, music or other interests

Be a good role model

Set a good example

Be honest when you get things wrong

Respect yourself

Look after your health

Have your own interests, aims and ambitions

Activity sheet – Parents against drugs

Parenting in action

Being a good parent is not easy. Read the guidelines on the Resource sheet, 'How to be a good parent'.

 Now look at the stories below. For each one, discuss which guideline is being broken or followed.

'Why don't you invite Paul round to join us for dinner?'

This parent is following/breaking the rule to _____

2

'You're over an hour late and you didn't phone so you can forget going out tonight.'

This parent is following/breaking the rule to _____

3

'You look… er… great.'

This parent is following/breaking the rule to _____

4

'Don't talk rubbish. You don't know what you're talking about.'

This parent is following/breaking the rule to _____

5

'Is that Gemma's mum? I'm just phoning up to check that my daughter, Ellen, is at your house. She said she would be.'

This parent is following/breaking the rule to _____

Teacher's notes

Alcohol, drugs, cigarettes and pregnancy

Objectives

- To understand how substances pass from the mother to an unborn child
- To learn about the dangers of alcohol, smoking and drugs during pregnancy

Prior knowledge

Students require a basic knowledge that drugs, alcohol and tobacco can be harmful.

Links to the PSHE: Personal Well-being KS3 Programme of Study for England

1.2   Healthy lifestyles
1.3   Risk

Links to the Draft Curriculum for Excellence for Scotland

Health and Well-being: Substance misuse

Links to the Personal and Social Education Framework for Wales

Emotional aspect
Moral aspect
Physical aspect

Links to the Learning for Life and Work: Personal Development requirements for Northern Ireland

Personal health
Self-awareness

Starter activity

Draw an outline of a pregnant woman on the board showing the womb, placenta, umbilical cord and baby. Ask students to name the parts correctly.

Resource sheets and Activity sheets

The Resource sheet, 'Sharing everything', can be used in conjunction with any of the Activity sheets in this section to show how substances pass from the mother to an unborn baby. The next three Activity sheets then look at smoking, alcohol and drugs individually.

All of the statements on the Activity sheet, 'Drugs and pregnancy', are true except for numbers four, five and ten. Although few studies have been carried out, it is thought that smoking cannabis carries the same risks as smoking tobacco. Most over-the-counter remedies are not recommended for pregnant women. Most prescription drugs are not recommended either and a doctor's advice should be sought before taking any medicines or alternative remedies.

Plenary

Students could come up with a list of five 'dos' and five 'don'ts' for a healthy pregnancy.

Background

Despite overwhelming evidence that smoking can harm unborn babies, a government survey in 2005 found that 17% of pregnant women still smoked during pregnancy. Numbers do appear to be falling though, since the figure in 1995 was 23%. The effects of illegal drugs on unborn babies are more difficult to identify as many women taking illegal drugs take more than one drug or also smoke and drink alcohol, making it difficult to attribute specific problems to particular drugs. There can be no doubt, however, that taking illegal drugs during pregnancy can be harmful, as can taking many legal drugs.

Resource sheet – Alcohol, drugs, cigarettes and pregnancy

Sharing everything

Look at the diagram below. It shows how anything the mother eats, smokes, drinks or takes in any other form is shared with her baby. This includes healthy things like oxygen and nutrients. It also includes dangerous things such as drugs, alcohol and the chemicals found in tobacco.

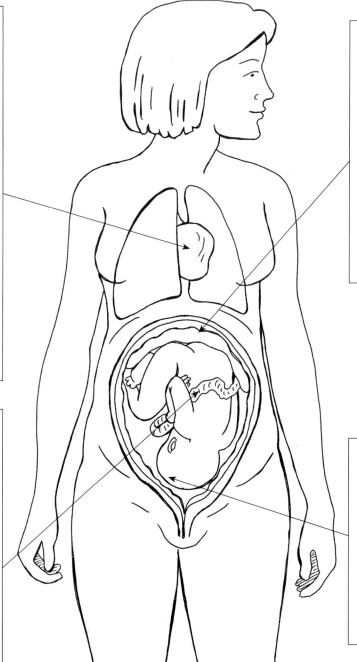

1. Chemicals from anything the mother smokes, eats, drinks or takes in any other way are absorbed into the mother's blood stream and pumped around the body by her heart.

2. The mother's blood flows through the lining of the womb and any substances in it are absorbed into the blood in the placenta.

3. The blood from the placenta is carried through the umbilical cord to the baby. It still has the substances in it that have been absorbed from the mother's blood.

4. The blood flows around the baby's body and brain before returning to the placenta.

Activity sheet – Alcohol, drugs, cigarettes and pregnancy

Smoking and pregnancy

Look at the Resource sheet, 'Sharing everything'. When a pregnant woman smokes, the chemicals she inhales are shared with her baby. Many of those chemicals are poisonous.

☞ 1 Find out what smoking can do to unborn babies by filling in the gaps in the paragraph below. Use the words from the box underneath the task to help you.

If you smoke when you are pregnant you are _____ likely to have a miscarriage or a _____ (where the baby is born dead). You are also more likely to have a small baby and small babies _____ from more illnesses and are more likely to have _____. Babies whose mothers and _____ smoke are also more likely to die from _____ deaths. Babies whose mothers smoked when they were pregnant tend to have more breathing problems and are more likely to develop _____. Every time you smoke when you are pregnant, your baby's _____ supply is disrupted for 15 seconds and the baby has a reduced blood _____ for 15 minutes.

Of course, many women smoke and go on to have perfectly healthy babies but why take the _____ ?

suffer	asthma	risk
cot	stillbirth	more
flow	disabilities	oxygen	fathers

☞ 2 Using the facts on this sheet, design a poster explaining why women should avoid smoking when pregnant.

Drugs

Alcohol and pregnancy

Emma is six months pregnant. Read her diary entry.

I can't stop worrying. Today I've been looking at a website about Foetal Alcohol Spectrum Disorder. It's terrifying. Apparently, if you drink heavily when you are pregnant your baby can have a low IQ, learning difficulties, problems concentrating, sight and hearing problems, heart trouble, liver damage, kidney problems, a deformed face, disabilities and so on and so on. The list is endless. I was really drunk when I got pregnant and I've had the odd glass of wine since too. The government isn't much help either. They say that pregnant women shouldn't drink at all but that if they do drink they should limit it to one or two units once or twice a week. So is it safe to drink or not? I wish I'd never looked at that website.

☞ Most of what Emma has read only applies to women who drink heavily but she is confused about what she should do. Help Emma out by matching the sentence halves to give her advice on what she should do while she is pregnant.

Pregnant women should definitely avoid	have one drink once or twice a week
Pregnant women should definitely avoid	pregnant women don't drink at all
Pregnant women are probably safe to	getting drunk
The government recommends that	drinking every day

Drugs

Activity sheet – Alcohol, drugs, cigarettes and pregnancy

Drugs and pregnancy

☞ Read the statements below and tick true or false to show whether you think each one is true or not.

		True	False
1	Taking ecstasy when you are pregnant can cause the baby to have limb and heart defects.	☐	☐
2	Babies of mothers who took heroin when they were pregnant can suffer from withdrawal symptoms when they are born.	☐	☐
3	Taking cocaine when you are pregnant can cause miscarriages, brain damage or death to the unborn baby.	☐	☐
4	Smoking cannabis when pregnant is safer than smoking cigarettes.	☐	☐
5	Pregnant women can safely use any over-the-counter medicine.	☐	☐
6	Pregnant women can safely use acupuncture.	☐	☐
7	Pregnant women should check with their doctor before taking any herbal remedies, vitamins or tonics.	☐	☐
8	Drugs can be passed to babies through breast milk.	☐	☐
9	The effects of many drugs on unborn babies are still unknown.	☐	☐
10	Most prescription drugs are safe for pregnant women.	☐	☐

Assessment sheet – Drugs

✓ | Tick the box to show what applies to you.

	🙂	😐	🙁
I listen to the teacher			
I work well on my own			
I work well with a partner			
I work well in a group			
I can give my own opinion			
I can give a presentation			
I listen to the views of others			
I can look for information			
I can present my work in a way that others can understand			
I can show sympathy and concern for others			
I can understand the good and bad things which people face in their lives			

My targets are:

1 _____

2 _____

3 _____